Index

Chapter 1: The State of Our Planet

Introduction

The Environmental Crisis

Climate Change

Deforestation

Pollution

The Destruction of Wildlife and Marine Ecosystems

How These Issues Are Interconnected

Chapter 2: The Causes of Environmental Problems

Introduction

Human Impact on the Environment

Overconsumption

Unsustainable Practices

Political and Economic Factors

The Role of Corporations

The Need for Individual Action

Chapter 3: The Effects of Environmental Problems

Introduction

The Impact on Human Health

The Impact on Biodiversity

The Impact on Natural Resources

The Impact on Climate

The Economic Impact

Chapter 4: Solutions to Environmental Problems

Introduction

Individual Actions

Sustainable Practices

Advocating for Policy Change

Direct Action

Corporate Responsibility

International Cooperation

Chapter 5: Animals and Wildlife

Introduction

The Importance of Biodiversity

The Impact of Human Activities

Threatened Species

The Role of Conservation

Chapter 6: Oceans and Their Animals

Introduction

The Importance of Oceans

The Impact of Human Activities

Threatened Marine Species

The Role of Conservation

Conclusion

Our Responsibility to Protect the Environment

Taking Action to Create a Sustainable Future.

Climate change is one of the most significant challenges facing our planet today. It refers to the long-term changes in weather patterns and temperatures that are happening globally. In this chapter, we will explore the causes and effects of climate change in more detail.

Greenhouse gases and the greenhouse effect

Greenhouse gases are gases in the atmosphere that trap heat from the sun, leading to an increase in global temperatures. The primary greenhouse gases are carbon dioxide (CO_2), methane (CH_4), and nitrous oxide (N_2O). These gases are released into the atmosphere by human activities such as burning fossil fuels, deforestation, and agriculture.

The greenhouse effect is a natural process that occurs when these gases absorb heat from the sun and radiate it back to the earth's surface. This process helps to keep the earth's temperature stable and habitable. However, when the concentration of these gases in the atmosphere increases, the greenhouse effect becomes stronger, leading to an increase in global temperatures.

Impacts of climate change

The impacts of climate change are far-reaching and include:

a)   Rising sea levels

Rising sea levels are one of the most significant impacts of climate change. As the earth's temperature increases, the polar ice caps melt, causing sea levels to rise. This can lead to flooding in coastal areas and the displacement of millions of people.

b)   More frequent and severe weather events

Climate change is also causing more frequent and severe weather events such as hurricanes, droughts, floods, and wildfires. These events can cause significant damage to infrastructure and agriculture, leading to economic losses and human suffering.

c)   Changes in ecosystems and biodiversity

Climate change is also affecting ecosystems and biodiversity. As temperatures rise, many species are being forced to migrate to cooler areas or are becoming extinct. This can have significant impacts on food chains and ecosystems.

d)   Human health

Climate change can also have significant impacts on human health. Extreme weather events such as heatwaves can lead to heat-related illnesses and death, particularly among vulnerable populations such as the elderly and children. Climate change can also lead to the spread of diseases such as malaria and dengue fever.

Chapter 2: Solutions to Climate Change

While the causes and effects of climate change are complex, there are solutions that can help reduce greenhouse gas emissions and mitigate the effects of global warming. In this chapter, we will delve into some of the solutions and actions we can take to address the problem.

Reduce greenhouse gas emissions

Reducing greenhouse gas emissions is essential to mitigate global warming. This can be achieved in several ways, such as implementing public policies, transitioning to renewable energy sources, and improving energy efficiency.

A)   Public policies

Public policies can be an effective way to reduce greenhouse gas emissions. Policies that incentivize emissions reductions, such as carbon taxes and emissions trading systems, can be effective in reducing greenhouse gas emissions.

In addition, policies that promote the use of renewable energy sources, such as subsidies for solar and wind energy, can help reduce greenhouse gas emissions.

b) Renewable energy

Transitioning to renewable energy sources, such as solar, wind, and hydroelectric power, can significantly reduce greenhouse gas emissions. Moreover, the development of renewable energy technologies has made these sources of energy more accessible and cost-effective.

c) Energy efficiency

Improving energy efficiency in buildings and transportation can reduce the amount of energy used and, therefore, the emissions generated. This can be achieved through the use of more efficient technologies, such as LED lighting systems, high-efficiency appliances, and electric vehicles.

Adaptation to Climate Change

In addition to reducing greenhouse gas emissions, we also need to adapt to the impacts of climate change that are already happening. This involves taking actions to reduce the vulnerability of communities to climate change impacts and building resilience to withstand future impacts.

a)   Building resilience

Building resilience involves taking actions to reduce the vulnerability of communities to climate change impacts. This can involve measures such as building sea walls to protect against rising sea levels, implementing drought-resistant agriculture practices, and improving disaster preparedness and response.

b)   Sustainable land use

Sustainable land use practices can also help to mitigate the effects of climate change. This can involve measures such as reforestation, sustainable agriculture practices, and the conservation of natural ecosystems. These practices can help to reduce greenhouse gas emissions and increase carbon sequestration.

c)   Sustainable transportation

Improving transportation infrastructure and promoting sustainable transportation modes, such as public transportation, walking, and biking, can also help to reduce greenhouse gas emissions and improve air quality.

3. Individual Actions

Individual actions are also essential to addressing climate change. While global action is necessary to reduce greenhouse gas emissions and adapt to climate change impacts, individual actions can also make a difference.

a)   Reducing energy consumption

Individuals can reduce energy consumption by turning off lights and appliances when not in use, choosing energy-efficient appliances, and using public transportation, walking, or biking instead of driving alone.

b)   Eating a plant-based diet

Eating a plant-based diet or reducing meat consumption can also help to reduce greenhouse gas emissions. Animal agriculture is a significant contributor to greenhouse gas emissions, and reducing meat consumption can have a significant impact on emissions reduction.

c)   Supporting sustainable businesses

Supporting businesses and organizations that prioritize sustainability and environmental stewardship can also make a difference. By choosing to purchase products and services from companies that are committed to reducing their environmental impact, individuals can help to drive positive change.

4. Policy Solutions

In addition to individual actions, policy solutions are also essential to addressing climate change. Governments and policymakers at all levels must take action to reduce greenhouse gas emissions and promote sustainable practices.

A) Carbon pricing

Carbon pricing is a policy solution that can help to reduce greenhouse gas emissions. This involves putting a price on carbon emissions, either through a carbon tax or a cap-and-trade system. By making carbon emissions more expensive, carbon pricing can encourage businesses and individuals to reduce their emissions.

b) Renewable energy incentives

Governments can also incentivize the transition to renewable energy sources such as wind and solar power. This can involve measures such as tax credits, feed-in tariffs, and renewable portfolio standards. By making renewable energy more affordable and accessible, governments can help to accelerate the transition away from fossil fuels.

d)   Energy efficiency standards

Energy efficiency standards can also help to reduce greenhouse gas emissions by requiring businesses and individuals to use more energy-efficient products and practices. This can involve standards for appliances, buildings, and transportation, among others.

e)   International cooperation

Finally, international cooperation is essential to addressing climate change. The Paris Agreement, signed by 195 countries, is a critical step in global efforts to reduce greenhouse gas emissions and limit the impacts of climate change. Continued international cooperation and coordination will be necessary to ensure a sustainable future for all.

5. Impact on Marine Life

Marine life is particularly vulnerable to the impacts of climate change, with rising temperatures and changes in ocean chemistry disrupting the delicate balance of the ocean ecosystem. Here are some additional details about the impact of climate change on marine life:

A) Ocean acidification

As atmospheric carbon dioxide levels increase, the oceans are absorbing more CO2, which is causing the pH of the ocean to decrease. This process, known as ocean acidification, has significant implications for marine life. The increased acidity can make it difficult for some species to form shells or skeletons, making them more vulnerable to predation and other stresses.

b) Changes in ocean currents

Rising temperatures are causing changes in ocean currents, which can have a ripple effect on marine ecosystems. Changes in ocean currents can alter the distribution of plankton and other organisms that form the base of the food chain. This, in turn, can impact the abundance and distribution of larger marine species, including fish and whales.

d)   Coral reefs

Coral reefs are some of the most biodiverse ecosystems on the planet and are home to countless species of fish, plants, and other marine life. However, climate change is causing coral bleaching, which occurs when the water becomes too warm for the coral to survive. Coral bleaching can lead to the death of entire coral reefs, which can have significant impacts on the marine life that depend on them.

e)   Migration and reproduction

Climate change is affecting the migration and reproductive patterns of many marine species. For example, rising temperatures can cause some fish species to migrate to cooler waters, which can impact the balance of the ecosystem in both the areas they leave and the areas they migrate to. Changes in temperature can also impact the timing of reproduction for many marine species, which can impact the survival of their offspring.

6. Impact on Animals

Climate change is having a significant impact on animal populations around the world. Here are some additional details about the impact of climate change on animals:

A) Polar bears

As mentioned earlier, polar bears are one of the most iconic animals impacted by climate change. With the Arctic sea ice melting, polar bears are losing their habitat and access to food, which can lead to declining populations and even extinction.

b) Birds

Changes in temperature and precipitation patterns are altering the timing of migration and breeding for many bird species. This can have significant impacts on their survival and reproductive success. Additionally, some bird species are losing their habitat due to changes in vegetation patterns and the availability of food.

c) Mammals

Rising temperatures and changes in weather patterns are affecting the distribution and survival of many mammal species. For example, some species of rodents and hares are being forced to migrate to higher elevations in search of cooler temperatures, which can impact the availability of food and their ability to avoid predators.

e)   Insects

Climate change is also affecting the distribution and behavior of many insect species. Changes in temperature can impact the timing of life cycles, such as when insects emerge from hibernation or lay eggs. This can impact the survival and reproductive success of the insects, as well as the animals that depend on them for food.

Conclusion

In conclusion, we have explored the various pressing environmental issues facing our planet today, including climate change, deforestation, pollution, and the destruction of wildlife and marine ecosystems. We have seen how these problems are all interconnected, and how our actions as individuals and as a society have contributed to their severity.

However, it is not all doom and gloom. Throughout this book, we have also highlighted the many solutions and actions that can be taken to address these issues. From reducing our carbon footprint and supporting sustainable practices, to advocating for policy change and taking direct action to protect wildlife and nature, there are many ways in which we can all make a positive impact.

It is up to us, as a global community, to take responsibility for the health and well-being of our planet and all its inhabitants. By working together and taking action now, we can create a sustainable future for ourselves and for generations to come. Let us take inspiration from the natural world and its resilience, and strive to make the world a better place for all life on earth.